I Believe:
40 Daily Readings
for the Purposeful Presbyterian

The Apostles' Creed

Editors
Frank T. Hainer
Mark D. Hinds
Writer
Allan Janssen
Art Director
Jeanne Williams
Cover Design
Rebecca Hirsch

Published by Witherspoon Press, a ministry of the General Assembly Council, Presbyterian Church (U.S.A.), 100 Witherspoon St., Louisville, Kentucky.

PRINTED IN CANADA

www.pcusa.org/witherspoon

I Believe:
40 Daily Readings
for the Purposeful Presbyterian

The Apostles' Creed

Introduction

If a nonbeliever asked you what you believe, what would you say? A good place to start would be the Apostles' Creed. All Christians share the Creed; we say it together, many of us weekly; and it summarizes the faith in a few words.

Even as we recite these well-worn words, however, we may admit that we don't understand them well enough to answer the questions that would certainly come from the nonbeliever. The language of the creed sometimes sounds foreign and antiquated.

The Reformed branch of the church has sought to restate the faith in new vocabularies that meet the circumstances of a particular era. Presbyterian readers will be familiar with that practice; the Presbyterian Church has within the last forty-one years added two confessions to its Book of Confessions: The Confession of 1967 and A Brief Statement of Faith. The Theological Declaration of Barmen of the 1930s, written in the face of the rise of National Socialism in Germany, and the Belhar Confession of the 1980s, a South African confession written in the context of apartheid, are additional examples. The Reformed have ever understood that God's Word intersects with human history such that it calls forth a confessional response that clearly states what the church believes against the press of issues that call faith into question.

The church will use language that communicates within the context of its age. And yet we return to a creed that speaks in language that hails from the earliest centuries of the church's life. The words echo from deep places. Still, they puzzle us, cause us pause, and sometimes startle us to wonder whether we can understand, much less agree. So we study the creed, if only to understand its vocabulary, to clarify just what is being claimed, and to learn what it might say.

By reading this book you have embarked upon a disciplined study of the creed over the next forty days. The daily readings that follow are designed for individual study and reflection. Perhaps you observe a regular devotional time during your day; these readings could provide content for that important time.

For those who wish to reflect on these readings in a group setting, a small group study guide is offered on pages 57–80 of this book.

"I Believe"

Apostles' Creed

I believe in God the Father Almighty, Maker of heaven and earth,

And in Jesus Christ his only Son our Lord;
  who was conceived by the Holy Ghost,
  born of the Virgin Mary,
  suffered under Pontius Pilate,
  was crucified, dead, and buried;
he descended into hell;
  the third day he rose again from the dead;
  he ascended into heaven,
  and sitteth on the right hand of God the Father Almighty;
from thence he shall come to judge the quick and the dead.

I believe in the Holy Ghost;
  the holy catholic Church;
  the communion of saints;
  the forgiveness of sins;
  the resurrection of the body;
  and the life everlasting. Amen.[1]

---

1. *The Book of Confessions* (Louisville: Office of the General Assembly, Presbyterian Church [U.S.A.], 2004), 7.

iBelieve

Credo

Christians have been confessing from the beginning, voicing creeds. It's how the term "creed" originated: *credo*, I believe. We say it out loud, in public, in what or in whom we place our final trust. This is not just antique language and ancient ideas. Any time you encounter what the church teaches, you must ask yourself: Do I believe that? Another question is: What does it matter? What's at stake in our believing, for ourselves and for the world?

A creed is not Scripture, which is the witness to God's activity, nor is it the experience of God. Rather, a creed tries to put in words the implications of our experience of God. The experience of God demands articulation. A creed helps us do that. What we believe and what the church teaches matter a great deal.

The Apostles' Creed is the worshipful articulation of the church's trust in the particular God who calls it into being and whose story is told in the church's Scripture. In uttering the creed, the believer enters the great story of God's way with the world.

All language about God is inadequate. God is, truly, ineffable—that is, beyond words. We speak only to keep from remaining silent. We confess and worship the God who meets us, not as idea, concept, force, or even as the principle of being itself, but personally.

A Baptismal Creed

The church formed its creed as a way of distinguishing itself from an alternative form of belief. Christianity was born into a world suffused with religion, even religious fervor.

A particular "set" of religions pressed particularly hard against the fledgling faith. These go by the term *gnostic*. Although Gnosticism was a complex form of religiosity, we must attempt to describe it briefly, for Gnosticism was not only a major competitor with Christianity; many who entered the church came with a gnostic understanding and tried to interpret the faith within the categories of their former faith.

The Greek term means "knowing"; gnostics claimed to possess a secret knowledge of the ways of heaven and earth. Gnosticism was committed to a transcendent god who was reflected through a series of lesser deities. This supreme god was divorced from the lower world of matter, which a lesser sort of deity had created.

Some forms of Gnosticism believed in a Redeemer, a figure of light, who came to save humans from the corrupt world of matter. This Redeemer's presence was only apparently human, for the human form was too earthly for one who partook of the divine substance. The "saved" were rescued from this dark and sad world as they were initiated into the light of gnosis, or secret knowledge of revelation, beyond reason and faith.

Gnosticism also describes a general religious worldview, alive and well today, and even in Christian circles. Study the following heretical statements; if you've heard these, you might have been in the presence of a Gnostic:

Jesus was a Redeemer figure, human in appearance only. The world and all physical matter are evil from creation. The human's goal is to escape the body. Baptism, an initiation into a secret discipline, is just such an escape from this life and the beginning of a journey beyond this creation.

Against these beliefs, the church began to formulate a belief statement. The creed was a short way of stating the essentials of this young faith. In the second century, Hippolytus of Rome had written down a Greek "apostolic tradition" in the form of questions put to new believers about to be baptized. Scholars have traced the skeleton of the Apostles' Creed to these questions.

Thus, the Apostles' Creed forms the faith in which we are baptized and informs our stand against other claims to our allegiance. Through our lives, as God calls us to ever new commitments of faith, we return to the creed, to reclaim our identities as God's beloved.

Day 4 Whom Do You Trust?

The Gospel of Matthew ends with Jesus' injunction to his disciples: "Go therefore and make disciples of all nations, baptizing them in the name of the Father and of the Son and of the Holy Spirit . . ." (*Matt. 28:19*). The church was doing just that. It had taken root in the nations; and now it was baptizing in the triune name. "I believe" in the God whose name is "Father, Son, and Holy Spirit."

The creed, then, is an expression of trust, and that trust is placed not in a dogma, not in a religious system, not in a set of ideas, not even in a particular way of life. It is trust placed in an other. It is much as a child trusts her parent with her life; or a friend trusts friend.

Still, that other is not an unspecified "other." A groom doesn't pledge his life to a "bride," as if any old (or young) bride will do. He places his future, any children that will come, and his dreams with a particular person. It is the *name* that counts; the name is part and parcel of this person.

The baptized who made the creed her own, then, was not simply agreeing that "God exists." Her world was filled with many gods. Nor was she admitting to being religious; her neighbors were likely as religious as she. She was staking her life on a particular God, named as Father, Son, and Holy Spirit. She did not simply believe *that* certain assertions about God are so; she believed *in*, she gave herself to, this other in trust.

The Creed as Story

Why is there no mention of the Bible or Scripture in the Apostles' Creed? The query arises especially from the Reformed corner of Protestantism, where we insist on Scripture as nothing less than the Word of God. Such Reformed confessions as the Second Helvetic, the Belgic Confession, and the Westminster Confession all have articles or chapters on Scripture as the Word of God.

In the creed, by contrast, the believer is *naming* the God in whom he trusts. And Scripture is *not* God, but the revelation of God through the stories about the actions of God. Scripture witnesses to this God, as does the creed. But Scripture cannot stand in God's place. The result would be idolatry, albeit an idolatry that has proved to be peculiarly attractive to the Reformed. Even if Scripture is not mentioned in the creed, if we do not say "I believe in" the Scripture, that doesn't make the Bible less important. The Bible is the story behind the Name. The old books record the remarkable ways of this particular God with a particular people.

Names are more than a handy means of identification. If we needed only a means of identification, we could be satisfied with Social Security numbers. A name comes with a story, as genealogists know and enjoy as they pursue surnames back through the generations, slowly building up a story. Maybe the McDougals fought old clan wars, found their way to North America from poverty, established a home on the frontier. Their story includes a saint and a scoundrel or two. Your family name tells your story, or part of it. Your given name, too, has a story. It comes with all the experiences, all the adventures, all the disappointments, all the friends and lovers and acquaintances that go into making you the particular person you've become.

Scripture tells the story of the God with this particular name, sometimes in creeds. Deuteronomy has Moses instructing Israel to recite this creed when bringing their first fruits to the altar:

> "A wandering Aramean was my ancestor; he went down into Egypt and lived there as an alien, few in number, and there he became a great nation, mighty and populous. When the Egyptians treated us harshly and afflicted us, by imposing hard labor upon us, we cried to the Lord, the God of our ancestors; the Lord heard our voice and saw our affliction, our toil, and our oppression. The Lord brought us out of Egypt with a mighty hand and an outstretched arm, with a terrifying display of power, and with signs and wonders; and he brought us into this place and gave us this land, a land flowing with milk and honey."
>
> *(Deut. 26:5–9)*

The confession is the story of Israel's liberation from Egypt and guidance to the promised land. Notice that the worshiper *names* the God who liberates. This is the God who disclosed the divine name to Moses at the burning bush, this name, Yahweh, the Lord.

God's name comes with a story, with a history. The creed tells that story in short form. God's story precedes the world's beginning: God is the "maker of heaven and earth." God's story reaches its historical center in the person of Jesus: The Son was "conceived by the Holy Ghost, born of the Virgin Mary, suffered under Pontius Pilate . . . ." God's story continues into the present: The Holy Spirit brings into being "the holy catholic Church . . . the forgiveness of sins." Indeed, it moves to a future in both the second and third articles as the Son will "come to judge the quick and the dead," and we shall enjoy the "resurrection of the body; and the life everlasting."

An Act of Worship

The creed's baptismal ancestry reminds us that the recitation of the creed is an act of worship. That too helps us to understand what's going on with the creed. It places the creed in the context of the community gathered by the Spirit before its God, lifting its prayers and singing its hymns.

The creed is first a profession of faith to the Other, to this particular God. We acknowledge to God that we are gathered in worship of the God who comes to us as the liberator of Israel, who disclosed himself most fully at the cross, and who breathes new life, new creation, into us. It's like saying "I love you" to our beloved. We commit ourselves in trust to this God.

In fact, if we remember that the creed emerges from baptism, it reminds us of our baptismal identity. There, we vowed to "reject evil" and to "renounce sin and the power of evil in your life and in the world." Thus, we repeat our promise to turn from all other powers that tempt us to trust, all other "gods" that promise blessedness if we but give them our fealty.

Second, we profess our faith before the world. Our worship is a public act. We identify ourselves with this God and so acknowledge that God calls us to a way of being and living that distinguishes itself from other paths.

To be church is to be "confessional." The historic Reformation churches, particularly the Reformed, identify themselves as confessional churches. When asked what we believe, we can point to the Heidelberg Catechism or the Westminster Confession. But to be confessional is deeper than adherence to the doctrinal writings of our forebears. We act, we confess. The accent is on the verb, not the noun.

$\mathcal{D}^{ay}_{7}$ I Commit

In the 1930s the Confessional Synod of the German Evangelical Church propounded the Theological Declaration of Barmen. The first article began: "Jesus Christ, as he is attested for us in Holy Scripture, is the one Word of God which we have to hear and which we have to trust and obey in life and in death." That hardly sounds controversial. Yet in the context of rising Nazism, the implication was clear. If Jesus is the "*one* Word of God which we have to hear" (emphasis added), then all other ideologies must fall away. To say this was to place the believer's life on the line.

Thus, when we say "I believe," we speak a word that does something powerful. Philosophers have identified what they call "performative utterances." That mouthful indicates certain statements we utter that make something happen even as we say them. For example, when we say "I promise," our very speaking those words makes it a promise. A couple pledging their troth at the altar are not simply reporting on the state of their emotional attraction and commitment. They set their lives in motion in a particular direction. Their very words will find fulfillment years later as they hang in with each other through the rough patches, or as one waits on the other in the long lingering twilight of life.

When we say "I believe," we do more than sign on to a set of doctrines put in place by the ancient church. We commit ourselves out loud and in public to the God named in the short story we recite. We acknowledge our baptismal identity, that we belong to this God and to no other.

"I Believe in God . . . the Father Almighty"

$\mathcal{D}$ay 8 The Apostles' Creed (Interrogative Form)

The oldest surviving baptismal liturgy, dating from about the year A.D. 200 (Hippolytus), describes the candidate standing in the water and affirming the faith by responding to three questions, each centering on a person of the Trinity. To each question, the candidate responds, "I believe," and after each response the candidate is immersed in the water or water is poured over the candidate. The candidate's profession of faith was made in the context of articulation of the faith into which the new Christian was entering, and by which he or she would be refashioned.

The interrogative form of the creed (below) is in keeping with the most ancient form of the Apostles' Creed noted above. Using it expresses the historic and universal faith of the church. The interrogative form is now the form that is used in baptism in many branches of the church.[1]

Do you believe in God, the Father Almighty?
I believe in God, the Father Almighty, creator of heaven and earth.
Do you believe in Jesus Christ?
I believe in Jesus Christ, God's only son, who was conceived by the Holy Spirit, born of the Virgin Mary, suffered under Pontius Pilate, was crucified, died, and buried; he descended to the dead. On the third day he ascended into heaven, he is seated at the right hand of the Father, and he will come to judge the living and the dead.
Do you believe in the Holy Spirit?
I believe in the Holy Spirit, the holy catholic church, the communion of saints, the forgiveness of sins, the resurrection of the body, and the life everlasting. Amen.

1. *The Companion to the Book of Common Worship*, ed. Peter C. Bower (Louisville: Geneva Press, 2003), 106–61.

Person, Not Concept

Christians confess God, the father of Jesus Christ, as the One who exercises power through benevolent care and whose love creates all that is and that shall be.

God is our beginning and our ending. We are set here to "glorify God and to enjoy him forever." Reformed worship begins by calling on God's name and ends with the blessing in God's name.

However, we are inclined to fill the concept "god" with our imaginings. As humans, we come up against the boundaries of thought and hope and longing. Philosophers talk about God as "the one of whom none greater can be conceived" (try it!). We then take that concept of God and apply it to what Scripture tells us about the God who freed Israel and who sent a Son to be the salvation of the world.

Instead of beginning with our notion of God, Scripture's stories introduce us to Jesus of Nazareth, to the Spirit, and to the Israel from whence these stories emerged. Now when we think of God, we think first of the One who is with us (the Spirit) and who disclosed a love that was fully among us, ushering in a kingdom, redeeming all creation through a death given in love (Jesus).

We worship a particular god, not god-ness in general. We worship the god with a name: Father, Son, and Holy Spirit. We confess a god who meets us as *person* and not as concept, idea, force, or even the principle of being itself. And this particular God has disclosed the divine self in a history that intersected and changed our history two millennia past and continues drawing us to God's future.

God in Christ

So who is the God who meets us in the person of Jesus? A second-century thinker named Marcion concluded that the God who meets us in Christ is the God who is pure love. But that posed a problem. The God whose stories we read in the Old Testament didn't appear to be a very loving sort at all. That God commanded the elimination of Israel's enemies. When, for example, Saul had the effrontery to show compassion, God withdrew the blessing of Saul's kingship. The Old Testament God exhibits anger and wrath, and is often portrayed as changing the divine mind at a whim. Marcion solved the problem by posing two different gods. The "bad" God of the old era was replaced by the loving God who meets us in Jesus Christ.

Although the church condemned Marcion as a heretic for such views, these views persist because they are attractive. Christians are heard often enough saying things like: "Jesus replaced the laws of the Old Testament." "With the coming of Jesus, we see that God isn't *really* like the Old Testament God." We solve our embarrassment over the violent and rough pictures of God in the first section of our Bible by consigning it at the least to a God who hasn't really gotten down to God's real business.

However, adopting that strategy has serious consequences. First, we fundamentally devalue the Old Testament. It becomes something less than the Word of God, less than the Scripture assumed, confessed, and cited by the New Testament. Second, we focus on a Jesus who fits our notion of love and not the Jesus of the Gospels themselves. We lose the Jesus whose love expresses itself in anger and in judgment. The Jesus who received children, lepers, and the outcast could also be unyielding, angry, and judgmental. Third, the notion of a "savior" God as distinct from a "creator" God devalues the material, the created order, in favor of what is wrongly called the more "spiritual." The goal of the human will then be to escape this mess put together by the lesser God.

Finally, and most important, by accepting the notion of a "worse" and a "better" God, we introduce an inappropriate division into God's identity. The church could not allow this sort of thinking even into speculative conversation for it was to deny the God who is not only present in Jesus Christ, but who *as father* is the Almighty One who created and creates.

Critics, often but not solely from a feminist perspective, have pointed out grave difficulties with speaking of God as "father." It is, for example, very difficult for a person who has known only an abusive or absent father to think of God as "father." That person brings to her or his relationship with God a picture of fatherhood counter to what is intended by Christian confession.

More serious, however, is the criticism that the notion of "father" imports male imagery into the very being of God. God, it follows, privileges one gender, the male, over the other; the male is ontologically, in the order of being, closer to the divine as male simply by virtue of chromosomes! God, of course, transcends gender, all would agree. Why, then, retain a gender-specific image in the church's liturgical, confessional, and doctrinal life? Critics can and often do continue to aver, often rightly, that Scripture itself betrays a hierarchical, male bias that need not be imported into contemporary life.

In fact, many of these same critics have pointed us to nonmale imagery of God. God is sometimes portrayed with *motherly* images. "Can a woman forget her nursing child?" *(Isa. 49:15)*. The picture can run deeper and more subtly. When God is confessed as merciful in *Ex. 34:6*, the text uses an abstract adjective derived from the Hebrew root that means "womb." God's compassion moves out of the divine "womblike" care, a non-male, motherly image par excellence!

Still, the church would face difficulty scuttling the image of God as "father" because we confess our trust in a personal God. While we must be vigilant not to think of God as limited by human capabilities of understanding, we know persons only as male or female; it's in the nature of personhood. And when we keep in mind that our confession is not only talk *about* God, but address *to* God, we understand that we address not an idea or a diffuse reality, but a Someone. And the creed allows us to address that someone as "father."

i$\mathcal{B}$elieve

Father Almighty

While Scripture includes female images of God (and, we must add, nonpersonal images as well: God is my "rock," for example, *Ps. 18:2*), it betrays a decided preference for "father." We are left with the resurrected Jesus' words at the close of Matthew's Gospel, where Jesus instructs the disciples to baptize the nations "in the name of the Father and of the Son and of the Holy Spirit" (*Matt. 28:19*). Scripture was written within a culture fundamentally biased toward the male; nonetheless, we may discover a usable power in the creed's address of God as "Father Almighty."

With the term *almighty* we are back in the neighborhood of a general idea of "god." For whatever else "god" is or might be, God must be powerful over everything, or so we think. Otherwise, God would not be God! It is when we come up against limits that we begin to mutter about something or someone who is greatest, and thus most powerful, or "almighty."

In a patriarchal culture, the mighty one is the father of the household, and by extension, the king. Indeed, given its cultural setting, Scripture could understand only the father as the one who protects the clan from threatening forces.

Just so, the terms *father* and *almighty* modify each other. The God who showed himself in the deeds of history—liberating a slave people, calling them into the elect community of Israel, leading them from the Holy Place—was almighty, but this was the almightiness of one who protected and loved. And the one who loved "like a father" was no minor deity; the one uttered "Yahweh" did not come to the end of limits. This god was not subject to the vagaries of time, space, death, and disease. This "father" knew no limits.

The Father of the Son

Jesus claimed that "whoever has seen me has seen the Father" (*John 14:9*). Jesus is the one who addresses God as "Father," or "Abba" in his prayer. We learn to project this "father" back into the stories of God with Israel, but the primary relationship is that between the one we address as the "father almighty" with the one we address as "his only begotten Son" (leaving aside for the moment the essential oneness of God).

Notice, though, that we spoke of this as a *relationship*. That is utterly crucial, for by so doing, we have entered the Trinitarian commitment of the earliest church, and indeed of the faith itself, for we address a God who is *in essence* love, and not simply love as an abstraction, nor even as a force. This is love between—we grope for words here—what the theological tradition named "persons." The first person of God is the one who loves into being and who continues to love. If we continue to use the term *father*, then at the least this transforms and transcends all human notions of "fatherhood."

But we must add more, for this relational commitment of God to the Son does not remain isolated to Jesus but includes all God's children. Paul reminds us in a sparkling Trinitarian passage that we have received "a spirit of adoption. When we cry 'Abba! Father!' it is that very Spirit bearing witness with our spirit that we are children of God" (*Rom. 8:15b–16*). Thus the God we confess is not just *any* "father almighty." This God functions in divine almightiness not by dint of sheer force that reflects the power of the Caesars (or the Pharaohs), but by a power that works through weakness, or, in Christian shorthand, the cross. This is power that doesn't destroy to save; rather, it is willing to be destroyed to save, and save even those who deserve eternal punishment, sinners. Confession of God as "father almighty" is not theological speculation, but joyful recitation of the living God who meets us in history to save us and all the world.

The Father Who Creates

We understand creation as an act of the same God who meets us in the Son. Creation, then, is an act of love. God calls creation into being out of love.

One could think that God created all that is as a sort of platform, a stage on which to be about the truly important divine work. God needed the stage sets and the players in place before the real business of the drama could get started; creation, on that notion, would be logically necessary.

But that can't be if creation *itself* is loved into being, if God delights in the very act of creation *and* in that which is created. To love another is to cherish him or her in that person's very existence, not for his or her utility. God delighted in creation. It is the product of divine love. It was, God said, "good, very good."

The God who created in love sends the Son, in love, to redeem *creation*. God would do no other, if the creation is God's beloved. Christian theology has focused for so long on the human person that it has lost contact with God's intention for creation.

But what, finally, does this say about God? If our creed confesses that God is the One who loves creation into existence, then what happens to and with creation *makes a difference to God*. God does not reside beyond the anguish and struggle of history, indifferent to what happens to God's creatures. God is passionately involved with history. And, in fact, Scripture presents us with just such an "odd" God who rages, who speaks tenderly, who assumes human flesh—all because this God cares deeply and loves long. The God who created the heavens and the earth began a long journey with the creation, one of love that would culminate at Golgotha and would stretch out until the end.

"I Believe in God . . .
the Crucified Messiah"

. . . Christ, Jesus,

    though he was in the form
        of God,
    did not regard equality with God
    as something to be exploited,
but emptied himself,
    taking the form of a slave,
    being born in human likeness.
And being found in human form,
he humbled himself
and became obedient to the point
        of death—
even death on a cross.

Therefore God also highly
        exalted him
    and gave him the name
    that is above every name,
so that at the name of Jesus
    every knee should bend,
    in heaven and on earth and
        under the earth,
and every tongue should confess
    that Jesus Christ is Lord,
    to the glory of God the Father.

iBelieve

The church confesses as Lord a human Messiah who announced the presence of God's reign. In this human's death, burial, and descent into hell, God disclosed the suffering one as God's beloved Son.

Robert Coles, the Harvard child psychologist, tells the story of Ruby Bridges, a young black girl who desegregated the New Orleans schools. As she walked to school through jeering crowds, Coles saw her lips move. When he asked her later what she was saying, she replied that she was praying. Coles asked her what she was praying, to which she answered: "Please, dear God, forgive those people, because they don't know what they're doing." This young girl in the 1960s was praying Jesus' own prayer from the cross! (See *Luke 23:34*.) At the center of her life stood a man who lived two millennia past.

When we confess the creed we claim the same center for our lives. Here we are at the heart of the creed, and of our faith. It's a remarkable claim: that we orient our lives around a man who lived a short life in the distant past. And yet we have been baptized in his name; we wrestle with what it means to follow him; we gather around his table in our central act of worship; we celebrate his birth, his death, and his resurrection in the great feasts that mark our faith. Who was—and is—this man? And what are we saying when we profess faith in him?

We begin by saying we believe in "Jesus." Like every other human, this Jesus lived a particular life. He was born into a particular history. He was a Jew. He fully entered the life of a people who counted their life from the Exodus from Egypt, who lived out of the stories of their Scripture, who were shaped by a Torah that created David's kingdom, and who had heard the prophets' strange call. He lived his life among a people who longed for freedom from Roman rule, and who bore in their memory promises of a new David, a Messiah.

$\mathcal{D}\text{ay}$ 17 Born, Suffered

Two phrases in the creed locate Jesus squarely in human history: "born of the Virgin Mary, suffered under Pontius Pilate." The idea of a virgin birth has been difficult for some to swallow, a biological miracle that demands a credulity modern sophisticates have outgrown along with knee-length bathing suits. In fact, some more conservative groups have made just this phrase a test of orthodoxy. While it is puzzling why the same folk who could accept the miracle of the creation itself, or of the incarnation (the Son of God becoming human flesh), find the notion of a miraculous conception beyond the pale, this phrase did not function in the creed originally to "prove" the divine nature of the child Jesus. It worked the other way around; this Jesus did not happen upon our earth in a manner different from that of any other human creature. He wasn't dropped from the sky, but was formed in the same way that each of us got started, cell dividing into ever more cells. Jesus is our brother, so to speak.

The "virgin" half of the phrase does indeed point to a wonder. But the surprise is not so much a divine sleight of hand done to impress us. It's much greater. It expresses divine love concretely, in the reality that is as intimate and as fundamental as the womb. It celebrates the God who could act against human impossibility. In the virgin birth, we celebrate not biology, but theology, the story of the God who comes nearer to us than we could have imagined. That's the true wonder.

If Jesus is born like us, from the intimacy of the womb, crying for his mother, playing with siblings, he likewise *suffered* with us. The context shifts from family to politics. History, our history, is littered with the victims of political and economic decisions: Sudanese refugees, Jewish inmates of the death camps, the underemployed crowded in our cities and hidden away in rural enclaves. The One who is the center of our faith did not escape suffering. In fact, as one very early hymnic confession put it, he *chose* the path of suffering: He "counted equality with God not a thing to be grasped, but humbled himself, taking the form of a slave" (see *Phil. 2:6–7*).

To confess "Jesus" is to say three things. First, the one we call Lord is our brother. This is a human who lived under the same limitations and sorrows as do we, death included.

Second, we indicate the *historical* character of our faith. To call faith historical is not only to say that God is concerned with human history. I might care deeply about the fate of African refugees, but I will express that care through financial contributions or political action. God doesn't act from a distance; God acts in history. And that action reached its fullest extent in the person of Jesus.

Thus, because God takes history with utter seriousness, Christians do too. Not only is it not our goal to escape the vagaries of historical existence; we recognize that God has purposes with history. This remains true even as we recognize that God has purposes beyond history.

Third, our faith is not caught up in a sort of vague religiosity. Ours is not a suspicion that there is "more." It's not a simple longing for a greater reality. It looks squarely to Jesus, a person who was born, who lived a particular human history, who wept, who laughed, who suffered disappointment and grief, who died, as we all will. I believe in this Jesus.

$\mathcal{D}$ay 18 Messiah

Who was this man? As the Gospel of Mark tells the story, Jesus put this very question to his disciples at the turning point of Mark's narrative: "Who do you say that I am?" Peter's reply echoes in our creed: "You are the Messiah." Or, as we alternatively translate it: "You are the Christ." Hence the creed: I believe in Jesus Christ.

"Christ," then, is not Jesus' second name (he did not come from a family named "Christ"); it is a title. It announces what this Jesus was about. Again, the Gospel of Mark provides the necessary clue when it opens with Jesus' own words: "Repent and believe, for the kingdom of God is at hand." The Messiah, the long-awaited new David, was thus to institute a kingdom. When we confess Jesus as Messiah, we point to the kingdom. The Messiah inaugurates this kingdom.

That fact meets a common criticism leveled against the creed's presentation of Jesus. Jesus' life and work, it is said, is reduced to a comma as the creed moves directly from Jesus' birth to his suffering under Pilate. What happened to the rest of the Gospel story? Well, the creed in fact sums it up in Jesus' title: We confess that Jesus is the Christ, the anointed One.

When we say "Jesus Christ," then, we make it startlingly clear that we trust that something new is happening in human history. We will point to signs of the kingdom that reflect the Gospel story: the feeding of the hungry, say, or the healing of the sick. We might point to signs of peace, where dividing walls come down (see *Eph. 2:14*). And we are saying that this is the *contemporary* work of the same Jesus who fed the five thousand and who healed the woman with the issue of blood.

A Death

The creed focuses on the death of Jesus, using several verbs to describe the event at Golgotha: "was crucified, dead, and buried; he descended into hell." While many believers may wish to concentrate on the life and work of Jesus, the earliest communities saw God's decisive act in Jesus' death. The Gospel stories themselves spend a disproportionate number of words on Jesus' final week. Indeed, the church's developing liturgical life centered on just this facet of Jesus' presence: In baptism the new believer ritually walked through Jesus' death, the water symbolizing the blood of the cross; and in the supper, the community proclaimed this death as it gathered around Jesus' broken body and shed blood.

But if his death was so important, what did it mean? And what does it tell us about the identity of this man? Here we stumble across another silent point in the creed. While it recites the story—crucifixion, death, burial—it does little to interpret it. Readers raised in the church will be familiar with what are called "theories of atonement." Perhaps the most familiar to Reformed folk has Jesus, in his death, taking our place, thereby "paying the price" for the sins we have committed (scriptural support for this view coming from, among other places, *Romans 3*). But that's not the only interpretation. The early church, for example, saw in Jesus' death his victory over the power of the evil one, over death, and over the power of sin. The creed appears to give no hint about which direction to take.

And yet the creed's sparse narrative ushers us into a startling history. This Jesus was *crucified*. Not simply a death, it was a certain kind of dying: Jesus was executed. That means that he was rejected by his society, condemned to take his place among those who were deemed to have no moral right to exist. Jesus was judged by humanity to be a criminal worthy of capital punishment. Some have suggested that for moderns to get the full impact of what happened, we ought to wear gold-plated electric chairs around our necks!

And who, says our creed, was this crucified Jesus? He was, and is, the only Son of God the Father Almighty. This one who became our brother, who lived in solidarity with us, is the deepest and highest expression of the love of God. This is God who went to the extremes, the God who entered fully into the life of the creature, and so became one with we who are—by definition, not God. The cross was the culmination of the human rejection of God, which terribly and paradoxically is also the human rejection of all that is best for us. Here what we call "sin" is disclosed in its full reality and horror; Jesus suffers the consequences of human sin.

Jesus' crucifixion, death, and burial (and yes, descent into the abode of the dead) was his full identification with all the victims of history's horrors, of human sin and evil. But it is more, for the Jesus we have confessed as Messiah did not stop being Messiah when condemned to the cross. The inscription at the cross, "King of the Jews," intended as irony, was true indeed. Just so, believers have held that this death was not the death of a heroic martyr, but was, in some indefinable way, a *saving* act of God. Thus, death and sin and suffering are not the final arbiters of history. Glory be to God!

The Son of God

Who is this man? It requires but a nodding acquaintance with Christianity to stumble across discussions about Jesus that attempt to put together "divinity" and "humanity." Jesus was both God and human. Indeed, the early church spent a good bit of energy (and not a small amount of bloodshed) over the question: In what way was Jesus both human and divine? Nor was this just an exciting intellectual puzzle. Believers were asking just how God intervened in human history in such a way that God both identified with us fully *and* had the power to save. The Nicene Creed would later begin to put it into words with phrases describing Jesus as "true God from true God, begotten, not made," and so on.

Interestingly, the Apostles' Creed says very little; it doesn't speculate on the relation of "divinity and humanity" in Jesus. It stays a bit closer to Scripture by using description rather than abstraction. It also simply indicates that this Jesus is God's "only Son."

We've purposely delayed consideration of the term *Son* to this point. That way, we have some idea of just who this Son is. It might be possible for you to think of someone's son without ever having come into contact with the son. You could speculate on what he must be like from what you know about the parent. However accurate your reflection, it had its starting point with the parent. But that doesn't work with God, for we've not seen God. And when Jesus' contemporaries exercised their imagination of what the Messiah must be, they failed not only badly, but dangerously.

The creed points to Jesus Christ and confesses that this One, who bears this name, is nothing less and nothing other than the Son of God! In so doing it says a number of things that are as surprising today as they were when the first anonymous authors put these words down.

First, we perceive in Scripture's story something quite astounding about *God*. It's easy for contemporary Christians to follow some early heresies and "factor out" the divine and the human in Jesus, ascribing the "god part" to such things as miracles, wise teaching, or Jesus' ability to outfox his opponents. Other attributes and experiences, the suffering, the dying, the questions Jesus presented, we ascribe to the human. Which is exactly backward! The Gospel of John tells us that Jesus' glory was the cross. In other words, when we see Jesus' suffering, we see God! This is who God is, the One who goes the full distance to human suffering.

This is God-with-us. We noted previously that the creed came into existence in a gnostic environment and set itself against those sorts of religious notions. The varieties of Gnosticism knew a redeemer figure that looked a lot like our Jesus. The difference was that their redeemer only *appeared* to be human (the heresy was called "Docetism" in distinction from Ebionitism that saw Jesus as no more than human). Not so for Christianity; this is God's Son, the One who went the full distance, descended into hell, we say.

Second, this is the particular God we worship. In this creed we express our worshipful trust in one who has a *name*. Here we meet the name in a fresh guise; the name is Jesus. Peter put it like this: "There is salvation in no one else, for there is no other name under heaven given among mortals by which we must be saved" *(Acts 4:12)*. The only hope we and the world have is in this particular, suffering, scandalous human—Jesus.

Our Lord

We find *ourselves* in the second article of the creed when we say "our Lord." The Holy Spirit wakens our hearts to utter this phrase.

> Therefore I want you to understand that no one speaking by the Spirit of God ever says "Let Jesus be cursed!" and no one can say "Jesus is Lord" except by the Holy Spirit.
>
> *(1 Cor. 12:3)*

It's important to reflect on the content of that confession. We aren't venturing into deep and difficult theological waters of *how* this Jesus is both our brother and the Son of God. That would become grist for the first century's Trinitarian developments. We simply stand in wonder. Like Thomas, we're confronted with the risen Christ who still carries the wounds of the cross, and we're left like him to confess "my Lord and my God!" *(John 20:28).*

Not only did Jesus display God's presence in places that were not high, but in the hellish places; among not only the pious, but among the sinners. Jesus is the God who triumphs through suffering and death. He is the One through whom we can pray for the victory of God's way over the powers of darkness that would consume us.

Prayer:
Eternal God,
your Son, Jesus Christ,
now exalted as Lord of all,
pours out his gifts on the church.
Grant us that unity which your Spirit gives,
keep us in the bond of peace,
and bring all creation to worship before your throne;
through Jesus Christ our Redeemer,
who lives and reigns with you in the unity of the Holy Spirit,
one God, now and forever. Amen.[1]

---

1. *Book of Common Worship* (Louisville: Westminster/John Knox Press, 1993), 206.

"I Believe in God . . .
the Resurrected Jesus"

The Third Day

The Apostles' Creed (Modern Version)

I believe in God, the Father almighty,
creator of heaven and earth.

I believe in Jesus Christ, God's only Son, our Lord,
who was conceived by the Holy Spirit,
born of the Virgin Mary,
suffered under Pontius Pilate,
was crucified, died, and was buried;
he descended to the dead.
On the third day he rose again;
he ascended into heaven,
he is seated at the right hand of the Father,
and he will come again to judge the living and the dead.

I believe in the Holy Spirit,
the holy catholic church,
the communion of saints,
the forgiveness of sins,
the resurrection of the body,
and the life everlasting. Amen.[1]

---

1. *Book of Common Worship* (Louisville: Westminster/John Knox Press, 1993), 65.

iBelieve

Raised Again from the Dead

Eighteenth-century Scottish philosopher David Hume taught us that miracles are impossible. They violate the universe, the naturally ordered. We are his skeptical heirs. We live the Enlightenment's heritage. Few of us would give up penicillin or toilets that flush. But that has made it difficult for us to accept statements about reality that do not fit the canons of knowledge given to us by science or logic.

Which makes it the more difficult as we move to the second half of the creed's second article. We do fine with the phrases about Jesus' birth and death (even though we may have swallowed hard over "born of the virgin"). That Jesus lived and walked among us gives us little trouble. We can go further to interpret, to "read into," his death a theological meaning of profound significance. Even more, we may even confess that this human Jesus was, in some sense, "divine." But when we reach the final phrases—descent into hell, resurrection, ascension, last judgment—we're in a new world, a different world. The "sidewalk ends." We've entered *terra incognita*, the unknown world. Such events are beyond our ken.

And yet none less than the great apostle admonishes his Corinthian correspondents: "If Christ has not been raised, your faith is futile and you are still in your sins" (*1 Cor. 15:17*).

It can't be verified scientifically; scientific confirmation requires repeatability. Jesus' resurrection was a one-of-a-kind occurrence. It also does not fit historically, or at least not very well. To understand any event, you must place the event in a category of some sort. The resurrection doesn't (and didn't) fit categories. By the nature of the case, attempts to "prove" or to "explain" Jesus' resurrection fall short.

And yet, we have inherited the witness of the apostles (recall that according to *Acts 1*, witness to the resurrection was a prerequisite to being named an "apostle"). We stand before the power of a reality, even if its contours and explanation escape our critical abilities.

The Person of Jesus

The tragic events at Golgotha could certainly have engraved Jesus in his followers' memory. His martyr's death could have sealed his kingdom project. Jesus left history with stories and actions that have captured our imagination ever since.

The early church could not leave matters at that. Jesus was also and essentially the resurrected One. The resurrection indicates something essential about the identity, or the person, of Jesus. Here we need to be clear on just what *resurrection* means. It is not another way of saying that Jesus was divinely immortal, as though his death was somehow a walk-through, with Jesus only playing a part. Jesus was mortal. It came with his birth. Resurrection means that Jesus was raised from the dead, *as a human*. God truly did go the distance; the Incarnation is not just a profound idea. It's real.

If Jesus was human, that means that he had a body, for to be human, essentially, means to be embodied. Many gnostics believed in a divine figure that came from heaven to release humans from the weight of their bodily imprisonment. Again we hear the anti-gnostic strains of the creed. It was a *bodily* resurrection.

Second, resurrection does not mean resuscitation from death. A resuscitated body—Lazarus would be a good example—will face death in its future. It's just been given a new lease. Jesus' resurrection was the conquering of death itself. When we confess Jesus' resurrection, we claim that this same human Jesus is alive, embodied, even now.

Thus, the resurrection stands not as proof of Jesus' inherent divinity, that somehow he had the "inner strength" to overcome even death. The resurrection confirms Jesus' utter humanity.

Raised with Christ

We should not be surprised by our difficulty with the resurrection, for we are up against something strange or *alien*. We stand before the wonder that is God! And God fits neither our expectations nor our demands of what a God should be like. While the person of Jesus as our brother means that God is with us, the resurrection testifies that it is God who is with us, in God's way.

Divine reality, and thus human salvation, does not emerge from the depths of nature. Death has the last say. All things that live die. While death may be a friend to the aged and ailing, it is, Paul reminds us, "the last enemy." Said simply: We can't save ourselves; and nothing else in all creation can save us either!

Jesus' resurrection, then, stands as witness that God breaks through everything. The early church considered the unholy trinity of sin, evil, and death as powers that destroyed not only humanity, but creation too. The resurrection proclaimed God's power over *all* authorities that claim allegiance because they have the power of death at their disposal. *Nothing* could stop God, through Jesus, from rescuing God's people.

For each believer, it comes with baptism. When speaking of baptism, Paul reminded the Romans that if we have been "united with [Christ] in a death like his, we will certainly be united with him in a resurrection like his" (*Rom. 6:5*). Our resurrection awaits us in the future, but it is already made certain in Jesus' resurrection.

It does not deny—rather, it confirms—our humanity. It confirms our *bodily* humanity. We are not ethereal souls, waiting to be liberated from an earthly "prison." Indeed, Jesus' resurrection does not give us license to flee present difficulties for a pleasant land beyond the grave. Instead, it confirms the fact that Jesus' reign is not otherworldly, but includes our life as we know it. We live confidently into a future where Jesus' death conquers the death that threatens all we hold dear. And because death cannot threaten, we live courageously in every new day.

$\mathcal{D}$ay 26   He Ascended

Since Jesus rose, the obvious question follows: Where is he? The assertion of the ascension answers clearly: The human, crucified Jesus is now bodily with God. (In fact, that's what all the commotion in the controversy over the Lord's Supper was all about in the sixteenth and seventeenth centuries. The Zwinglian Reformed maintained that since Jesus had bodily ascended, he could not be physically present in the Supper. Lutherans maintained that Jesus could be present "bodily" everywhere; his body was "ubiquitous." Calvin opted for a third way; Jesus was "spiritually present" in the Supper.)

Still, Jesus' ascension meant more than getting him offstage, something Jesus himself told his disciples was necessary for the coming of the promised Spirit. In his ascension, early believers understood that Jesus now stood before God as their advocate, as the great high priest who interceded on their behalf before God. This was the *human* Jesus, who walked with us in our anguish, who knew from the bottom up what it meant to live in the exigencies of time:

> Since, then, we have a great high priest who has passed through the heavens, Jesus, the Son of God, let us hold fast to our confession. For we do not have a high priest who is unable to sympathize with our weaknesses, but we have one who in every respect has been tested as we are, yet without sin.
>
> *(Heb. 4:14, 15)*

The Reformers emphasized this when, for example, the Genevan Catechism included among the "benefits" of Christ's ascension that "he appears before God as intercessor and advocate on our behalf."

In baptism we are united with Christ. Thus, in our union with Jesus, our human selves with all the hurts, all the brokenness, all the fear as well as the laughter enter God's presence in Jesus' ascension. Our confession is more than longing toward a future. It is a claim of what already *is*. Our life with God has already happened, in the person of Jesus.

i𝓑elieve

The Reign of the Messiah

While the confession of Jesus' ascension is profoundly comforting to believers, it contains awesome implications for our world as well. Paul put it thusly when speaking of the ascension:

> . . . God put this power to work in Christ when he raised him from the dead and seated him at his right hand in the heavenly places, far above all rule and authority and power and dominion, and above every name that is named, not only in this age but also in the age to come. And he has put all things under his feet and has made him the head over all things for the church . . . .
>
> (*Eph. 1:20–22*)

Jesus the Messiah ushers in a reign that has to do not only with a world "back then," but with our world as well. And not only with the souls of women and men, but with political and economic reality also. That reign has already begun, albeit in provisional form. The ascension points to the wonder that the governments, movements, economic forces, ideas, and science that rule over our world are not only limited in scope and power, but also bend to God's greater purpose. Thus, for example, believers could hold out against apartheid or slavery in the confidence that the Messiah not only will reign, but already *does* reign over the movements of history. Believers may be confident in the midst of ecological crises that even in and through the breakdown of our ecosystems, the Messiah reigns and will triumph. The confession in Jesus' ascension, difficult as it may be for the child of the Enlightenment, is anything but an antiquated item of belief to be shelved when the old picture of a three-story universe becomes inadequate.

Day 28 | To Judge the Living and the Dead

We remember Jesus' resurrection. We live in the present of Jesus' ascension. We anticipate, we expect that Jesus, seated at the right hand of God, will "come again to judge the living and the dead." We live "in the middle," in creation's history that is incomplete. The completion begins with Jesus as judge.

The church has too often used the last judgment as a club. We've frightened folk by placing them before the stern judgment of God where their sins will be brought to light. And whose life can stand God's examination? Admittedly, the church hoped that potential converts would then flee to the Jesus who accepted God's judgment on their behalf. Nonetheless, the notion continues to provoke the belief that we really must be on our guard lest we come to the final judgment unprepared. Do we readily enter the unknown future radically uncertain whether God has a place for us?

The judge is the same Jesus who came to proclaim God's righteousness: love for enemies; acceptance of the poor and the sinner; victory over sin, death, and evil. Thus, we anticipate judgment as a time of grace.

The judgment of the living and the dead speaks hope, especially for the victims of this world. If you see the world through the eyes of a victim, it looks as though raw power wins. The victor carries away the prize. The victim disappears into the mist. Indeed, the abuses of those in power fade into memory. When all has died, who will remember? Well, says this article of the creed, *God* remembers. God's memory is for the broken; it is not simply to punish the wrongdoer. Evil cannot triumph.

Still, God's judgment is more than memory. It continues the trajectory of God's action as we know it from Scripture's story. The Jesus who judges is the Christ of the cross. And the cross executed God's redemptive purpose on behalf of the wrongdoer!

Judgment signals transformation of even the wrongdoer, the bringing to God's right of everything and everyone: "through [Christ] God was pleased to reconcile to himself *all things*, whether on earth or in heaven, by making peace through the blood of his cross" (*Col. 1:20*; emphasis added).

Prayer:

God and Father of our Lord Jesus Christ,
you gave us your Son,
the beloved one who was rejected,
the Savior who appeared defeated.
Yet the mystery of his kingship illumines our lives.
Show us in his death the victory that crowns the ages,
and in his broken body
the love that unites heaven and earth.
We ask this through your Son, our Lord Jesus Christ,
who lives and reigns with you in the unity of the Holy Spirit,
one God, forever and ever. Amen.[1]

1. *Book of Common Worship* (Louisville: Westminster/John Knox Press, 1993), 395.

"I Believe in God . . . the Holy Spirit"

Day 29 Come, Holy Spirit

Come, Holy Spirit, our souls inspire,
And lighten with celestial fire;
Thou the anointing Spirit art,
Who dost Thy sevenfold gifts impart.

Thy blessed unction from above
Is comfort, life, and fire of love;
Enable with perpetual light
The dullness of our mortal sight.

Teach us to know the Father, Son
And Thee, of both, to be but one;
That through the ages all along
This may be our endless song:

Praise to Thine eternal merit,
Father, Son, and Holy Spirit.
Amen.[1]

"If you love me, you will keep my commandments. And I will ask the Father, and he will give you another Advocate, to be with you forever. This is the Spirit of truth, whom the world cannot receive, because it neither sees him nor knows him. You know him, because he abides with you, and he will be in you."

(*John 14:15–17*)

---

1. *The Presbyterian Hymnal* (Louisville: Westminster/John Knox Press, 1990), no. 125.

i*B*elieve

God's Promise

Scripture is a story of *promise*. God calls Abraham with a promise (*Gen. 12*). The revelation of God's name to Moses is a promise: "Yahweh" can best be translated as "I will be who I will be," or "I will be there as I will be there." Jesus promises his disciples at the end of Matthew's Gospel that "I am with you always, to the end of the age" (*Matt. 28:20*). And the entire story ends, "Amen. Come, Lord Jesus!" (*Rev. 22:20*). The Holy Spirit is the fulfillment of that promise to us: God is with us.

The Spirit is notoriously difficult to describe—and with reason. The word we translate as "spirit" comes from the Hebrew *ruach* and the Greek *pneuma*. Both words mean "wind" or "breath." The Spirit is the "breath of God." When God molded the first human from the mud, God jump-started the creature by breathing the breath of life, the *ruach*, into his nostrils (*Gen. 2:7*). Thus the human too was enlivened by Spirit.

But you can't see wind or breath. You can't pin either down and examine it. You can only perceive the effects. Treetops bend to the wind; a chest slowly expands and contracts to the movement of breath. We catch glimpses of God in our present as we grow into an awareness of the action of the Spirit. The Spirit is the "Lord, the giver of life" (Nicene Creed).

The God we confess does not demand that we live in a former era, as though we had to transport ourselves to first-century Palestine. Nor does this God call us to live in the ethereal realms of a spirit-world above this earthly plane, as though our families and our schools don't really count. One sees here the anti-gnostic tone of the Creed. God is with us. So we begin where we are, struggling through our marriages, wrestling with a consumer culture, pursuing our vocation, learning to live with neighbors who share a faith different from our own.

Day 31 | God Within

Our Reformed forebears talked about the *testimonium spiritus sancti internum*, the internal testimony of the Holy Spirit. God's Spirit addresses our spirit, as it were. What does that phrase mean?

You heard the old stories of Abraham and Sarah, Moses and Miriam, Jesus and Paul from the day your parents first told you. You listened to the preacher go on about Jeremiah and Anna. The stories may have interested you but only as tales of the past, probably with a moral attached. Then, at some point, the stories began to come alive. They became more than tales once told; they speak directly to you. *You* are in the story. The story calls to you. That is the internal testimony of the Spirit, God with you, God within you.

God wakens our hearts with divine breath; how will we respond? Will I place my trust in Jesus? Will I put my life in the hands of the rabbi from Nazareth? Faith is itself the gift of God (*Eph. 2:8*). It is not just what you believe but *that* you believe which points to the presence of the Spirit of God.

Here's a thought experiment: How did you come to faith in Jesus? What set of events converged to that point in your life where you could speak the creed out loud and in public? Some might point to a period of doubt or to a search for the sense of one's place in a confusing and dangerous world. What brought you through? Others can point to no particular moment; they were raised within the climate of belief, and their confession of trust was as natural as telling their parents that they love them. Still others might point to the stories of Scripture. Whatever your biography, whether you can identify your own Damascus road experience or your belief grew as you fought your way through adolescence, it is God's Spirit that has accompanied you and wakened you to faith.

Consider how we normally think of the group that identifies itself as a particular church—for example, the "Second Presbyterian Church." Our resolutely individualistic culture sees that body as a gathering of folk who *choose* the Presbyterian expression of Christianity. We constitute the church through our faith. And we maintain it through our commitment, our wisdom, our particular genius. But that's not what our creed claims. Whether you caught belief from your family or responded to an evangelist, you received the story from the "holy catholic church; the communion of saints." The church is the act of God.

The implications of that claim are immense and liberating. They are liberating because we do not need to create the communion that witnesses to the acts of God. God, through the Spirit, does so. The communion of saints is *itself* a contemporary act of God. You need only look around yourself. The gathering of the choir, the stories told in the church basement to little children, the youth group on its outing, the soup kitchen on the corner, and most of all the gathering of the community around pulpit and table are themselves the work of God right before our eyes and the eyes of all the world.

Even when the church's witness degenerates, when commitment has become paltry, even ludicrous, we do not lose heart, because we *believe* that God continues to work in and through this all-too-human institution called "church."

Prayer:
Almighty God,
you have knit together your elect in one communion and fellowship
in the mystical body of your Son, Christ our Lord.
Give us grace so to follow your blessed saints
in all virtuous and godly living that we may come to those ineffable joys
that you have prepared for those who truly love you;
through Jesus Christ our Savior,
who with you and the Holy Spirit lives and reigns,
one God, in glory everlasting. Amen.[1]

1. *Book of Common Worship* (Louisville: Westminster/John Knox Press, 1993), 386.

iBelieve

Day 33 Catholic

The wind of the Spirit that creates the church works through it to draw you within. The Spirit does so as it keeps the story alive. Even the most dedicated biblicist, the one who claims that he or she derives his or her belief from the Bible alone, cannot escape that fact, for while the Bible is God's gift to the church, the church hands the Book on from generation to generation.

What an extraordinary communion this is! It is, of course, that ordinary gathering that includes not only family and some friends, but the local banker, the physics teacher, the lonely waif who finds in the Sunday school a safe place, the aged, parents, young people. It includes the most committed believer, the half-doubter, and the seeker. The Spirit unites us with those who are not like us. Thus, are we drawn outside the little world we construct for ourselves into a relationship with those we're called to love. The Spirit draws us from our loneliness into a communion that is a taste of the full communion with God that is to be.

But this communion is not limited to the fellowship of the church we call "home." It's catholic; that is, it finds its home everywhere. When we sing the creed, when we lift our prayers, when we've gathered around the Lord's Table, the Spirit gathers us in communion with believers in Zaire, and Mumbai, and the South Bronx, and Grosse Pointe.

Nor is this communion of saints limited to the present. The Spirit unites us with the "church triumphant," those who live now with God. God's presence connects us with past and future. This is not only "our" church; it doesn't belong to those whose names currently fill the roll and who turn in pledge cards. It "belongs" only to God, and God draws us into a fellowship not only with the Augustines and the Teresas, but with our great-grandparents, and the ancestors of our Latin American sisters and brothers, too. And with our grandchildren!

Forgiven Sinners

Because this is a special communion, a communion of "saints," we easily delude ourselves into thinking that here, finally, we find ourselves in a community of perfect people.

The creed quickly disabuses us. The Spirit gathers us in the church as forgiven sinners. That brings us back to earth. This is not a group of folk who have somehow escaped the human condition. As a matter of fact, we are a most human people, confessing our entrapment in the awfulness of our own sin.

The church exists as a true communion, as the only true communion, because we have been forgiven. That is, the barriers we erect to love have been broken through by the only one who can break through them, God's act in Jesus Christ.

Why doesn't the creed speak of forgiveness in the context of the second article, under the work of Christ? In a strange but compelling story in Matthew, Jesus gives to Peter the "power of the keys." We Protestants have tended to avoid the story because our Roman Catholic neighbors have used it to defend the papacy. Just so, we have missed the implications of the story, for it grants the church the charter to proclaim forgiveness in the name of Christ. In the context of the creed, this follows naturally. The Spirit creates the church that communicates the story of Jesus; and in that story God addresses us with a forgiveness that reaches us where we live, in the very contexts where we withhold love, let anger run riot, and attempt to lift our lives out of the mire by the strength of our own character. Just so, the Spirit draws us into the communion where, in forgiveness, we can confess that God is with us.

Open to the Future

The forgiveness of sins opens us to God's future; we no longer live with the baggage of our past weighing us down. Still, the creed goes on to lead us to the very edges of our human existence as it confesses the "resurrection of the body and the life everlasting."

The creed is tilting against an old idea, one that is still with us. The creed was written at a time when it had been common for a very long time to believe in the immortality of the soul. It made sense to understand the soul as that peculiar entity that made us human. We were more or less accidentally burdened with a body. It was a religious task to discern an escape for the soul from matter, evil stuff that weighs us down. Immortality of the soul guaranteed that death could not destroy that which makes us human.

Scripture had quite a different understanding of the human person. The Spirit breathed life into the clay lump that God had shaped and so brought the human into existence. The human person was integral; it included both body and soul. They went together; remove either, and one is no longer human. Thus, the Easter Gospel talks not about immortality of the soul, but of the resurrection of the body.

This hits us where we live, for we live with our bodies. And our bodies wear out; we die. We live with death; we struggle through wrenching grief. Is this how it ends, with the loss of that which makes us particular, unique?

That's not Scripture's story! God loves us as the persons God created us, soul and body. The resurrection opened the hearts of the early believers to the wonder that the Spirit does not leave us desolate when we breathe our last. Paul reports that the resurrection means that we will receive a new body (what that will be escapes our imagining), but it is still a *body*! The Spirit will give breath to whatever form our life takes in a future we cannot conceive of.

Further Thoughts

Holy, holy, holy! Lord God Almighty!
Early in the morning our song shall rise to Thee;
Holy, holy, holy! merciful and mighty!
God in three Persons, blessed Trinity!

Holy, holy, holy! all the saints adore Thee,
Casting down their golden crowns around the glassy sea;
Cherubim and seraphim falling down before Thee,
Who wert, and art, and evermore shalt be.

Holy, holy, holy! though the darkness hide Thee,
Though the eye of sinfulness Thy glory may not see,
Only Thou art holy; there is none beside Thee
Perfect in power, in love and purity.

Holy, holy, holy! Lord God Almighty!
All Thy works shall praise Thy name, in earth and sky and sea;
Holy, holy, holy! merciful and mighty!
God in three Persons, blessed Trinity![1]

Prayer:
  O blessed Trinity,
  in whom we know the Maker of all things seen and unseen,
  the Savior of all both near and far:
  By your Spirit enable us so to worship your divine majesty,
  that with all the company of heaven
  we may magnify your glorious name, saying:
  Holy, holy, holy.
  Glory to you, O Lord most high. Amen. [2]

1. "Holy, Holy, Holy! Lord God Almighty!" *The Presbyterian Hymnal* (Louisville: Westminster/John Knox Press, 1990), no. 138.
2. *Book of Common Worship* (Louisville: Westminster/John Knox Press, 1993), 348.

iBelieve

An Act of the Church

Because the creed emerges from baptism, and because it is an act of worship, it is the *church's* creed. While we have no evidence that the creed has any connection with the original apostles, we identify it with them anyway. That's to our advantage, for we recognize that it articulates the foundational story as we have received it from its apostolic origin. It doesn't begin with you or me. It's the church's creed.

That fact helps us over a difficult hump. We live in a radically individualistic culture; it's bred into our bones. Our recent heritage taught us to doubt, to question everything that we can't verify for ourselves, or at least test if we had the ability and opportunity (few of us have seen an atom, let alone a black hole). That applies in our life of faith as well. So it's a problem when it comes to the creed. How can I confess that Jesus "descended into hell" and "sits at the right hand of the Father" when science has taught us that the universe is not three-storied? Or, more to the point, how can I confess a Holy Spirit when I don't know exactly what the creed is talking about?

It isn't my creed! It belongs to the church of the centuries. I add my voice to those who have gone before and to those who live beyond my culture and to children of future generations.

Reciting the creed is a profession of trust, a commitment to God. Take the matter of marriage. When a woman commits herself to a particular man (and vice versa), she has little understanding of what her commitment will mean, for she hardly knows her betrothed. They will reveal ever more of themselves as they live together through the years. They will grow into their vows.

And it isn't just that they will discover what those vows mean. The historic community has set those vows before them and all married people because the community knows more than they do what those vows will mean.

Likewise, we pledge ourselves with a community to a God who escapes our attempts to understand God's full story. But we do know that the mothers and fathers of the church have a broader and deeper understanding than we do of what God is about. We know that while we cannot always figure out why the virgin birth, for example, is so important, we trust that it expresses something essential, and may still do so. We have yet to grow into the full story.

Does that mean that we unthinkingly recite words that mean nothing to us? Of course not. While we are baptized into this faith, we are also educated into the story. Church school teachers teach us about Moses and David and Sarah and Ruth, Peter and the woman at the well, and Jesus. Our young people preparing to make public profession of faith attend classes. We teach those seeking to believe, to unite with the church, the beginnings of the story so that they might gladly join their voices to the creed. But we note too that this is only the beginning, as all of us grasp but the edges of the story.

Old Words, Timeless Word

The Apostles' Creed speaks in language that hails from the earliest centuries of the church's life. The words echo from deep places. Still, they puzzle us, cause us pause, and sometimes startle us to wonder whether we can still agree. So we study the creed, if only to understand its vocabulary, to clarify just what is being claimed, and to learn what it might say.

We continue to recite the creed. We do so because the Apostles' Creed is one of what we call the "ecumenical creeds." That is, its formulation precedes the great divisions within the church and the consequent particularities of later confessional documents. The Apostles' Creed is no more Lutheran or Roman Catholic than it is Reformed. It simply has nothing to do with the issues that divide us, as important as they may be. The creed unites us with sisters and brothers not only across confessional boundaries, but with the church of the first centuries. Likewise, as we allow the old creed its own way, we find ourselves able to articulate belief here at the beginning of the third millennium of the church's life. We have listened with open ears to fathers and mothers of the church, and in communion with them we listen afresh to Scripture's story.

Prayer:
God,
good beyond all that is good,
fair beyond all that is fair,
in you is calmness, peace, and concord.
Heal the dissensions that divide us from one another
and bring us back to a unity of love
bearing some likeness to your divine nature.
Through the embrace of love and the bonds of godly affection,
make us one in the Spirit
by your peace which makes all things peaceful.
We ask this through the grace, mercy, and tenderness
of your Son, Jesus Christ our Lord. Amen.[1]
—Dionysius of Alexandria (d. 264)

1. *Book of Common Worship* (Louisville: Westminster/John Knox Press, 1993), 812.

 iBelieve

Now, as we utter the word *God*, as we pray that name, we fully realize this as a *creed*. *Credo* is Latin for "I believe," or "I trust." I, we, place our trust in the One who in love called the world into existence. We trust this One who as almighty will not allow evil and death to triumph. This is the One who will be victorious not by the patterns familiar to us in the power that destroys in order to save, but who triumphs through a love that loses nothing and no one along the way. And, in fact, it is none less than the God who wakens within us the very ability to utter our prayer of trust. We believe in God the "Father Almighty" because we have been given to trust in the Son and through the Spirit. There a God meets us who cares for us and for all creation. Just so, a communion has persisted that sings this creed against all the powers, all the movements, all the ideals, nay, all the gods that claim our allegiance. *This* we believe, we say. *This One* we trust and worship, and to this God we pledge our love and fidelity.

> We all believe in one true God,
> Father, Son, and Holy Ghost,
> Ever-present help in need,
> Praised by all the heavenly host,
> By whose mighty power alone
> All is made and wrought and done.
>
> We all believe in Jesus Christ,
> Son of God and Mary's son,
> Who descended from His throne
> And for us salvation won,
> By whose cross and death are we
> Rescued from sin's misery.
>
> We all confess the Holy Ghost,
> Who from both fore'er proceeds,
> Who upholds and comforts us
> In all trials, fears, and needs.
> Blest and Holy Trinity,
> Praise forever be to Thee![1]

1. *The Presbyterian Hymnal* (Louisville: Westminster/John Knox Press, 1990), 137.

iBelieve

I Believe:
40 Daily Readings
for the Purposeful Presbyterian

The Apostles' Creed

SMALL GROUP STUDY GUIDE
By Carol Wehrheim

Introduction

Core beliefs of the Christian church are considered in this study based on the Apostles' Creed. These ancient words, used as a baptismal confession by the early church, are still repeated thousands of years later around the world. Thus, this creed connects us not only to the saints through the ages, but also to Christians of all theologies in every nation. Many congregations include the Apostles' Creed in the weekly service of worship, occasionally substituting other statements of belief. Who knows how many confirmation students have memorized the Apostles' Creed!

As a confessional church in the Reformed tradition, we profess our belief with this statement as a way to counter the ways of the world and to remind us of the centrality of our faith, no matter what issues or troubles unsettle us. This briefest of creeds contains clues to the beliefs that are at the heart of our faith. It is to the breadth of the biblical message as a time line is to the sweep of the history text. Each line brings to mind stories and Bible verses that we have heard, memorized, or read, perhaps for many years. Still, examining the Apostles' Creed is no easy task. What appears to be so simple is layered with meanings, tangled messages, and insights.

The first session places the Apostles' Creed on the time line of the Christian community. You will want to be familiar with the gnostic beliefs of that time. You might research this heresy of the early church by reading about it in an encyclopedia or church history text. *The Anchor Bible Dictionary* (Garden City, NY: Doubleday, 1992) allots several pages to this dualistic thought. Or ask a historian or an ancient-history buff to make a five-minute presentation (be definite about the length of time) to the group.

Session 2 is about the first two lines of the Apostles' Creed, signifying God as the creator of all and the source of love, a love revealed in Jesus Christ.

Moving to the middle of the creed, Session 3 focuses on the crucifixion and death of Jesus the Christ. You may need copies of A Brief Statement of Faith or another contemporary creed or confession for the group to compare to the Apostles' Creed. As you lead this session, try to keep the conversation centered on Jesus and the events prior to the resurrection, since the resurrected Christ is the primary focus of the next session.

Session 4 presents the real reason the Christian church came into being. Little in the creed's first references to Jesus would have created a community of believers long after the death of their leader; however, the resurrection causes us to see the life of Jesus through different eyes. Two concepts are featured in this session: resurrection and the judgment by Jesus.

The final session deals with the last section of the Apostles' Creed, which includes a reference to the Holy Spirit. The gift of the Holy Spirit to the believers at Pentecost is also available to believers today. As you prepare to lead this session, keep in mind today's spiritual climate. What are the desires of people as they pursue spiritual fulfillment? Watch for articles about spirituality in magazines or newspapers and bring them to the class. This session may be the most difficult one in the unit, if the participants think of the Holy Spirit as outside their religious experience or if the name of the Holy Spirit is spoken only in creeds. In that case, stress the role of the Holy Spirit in gaining and developing one's faith, as described in this study guide's plan for Session 5.

SMALL GROUP STUDY
For discussion of Days 1–7 in the daily reader;
to be used after Day 7

$\mathcal{S}$ession 1

"I Believe"

SESSION FOCUS

The Apostles' Creed brings us into the long history of the church, as we declare our trust in God, who has called it into being.

MAIN IDEAS

This study begins by locating the Apostles' Creed within the church's story, highlighting the gnostic context against which the creed was written. The emphasis is on the creed as a declaration of trust in a particular God—one who is named and addressed in the creed as Father, Son, and Spirit.

The emphasis on name has particular implications. First, the name distinguishes this God. Second, the name implies a story or a history. Furthermore, because the creed is an act of the church, the story is greater than the individual believer, and each must find her or his way into the story.

PREPARING TO LEAD

- Read the daily reader, Days 1–7.

- Write, or ask a calligrapher to letter, the Apostles' Creed (from Day 1) on one to three sheets of poster board that can be displayed in the meeting space throughout this study. Do not assume that everyone has memorized it, even those who have may not be able to recall a section without saying the entire creed. Using this contemporary version will give everyone an even footing.

- Explore the gnostic beliefs that prompted the writing of the Apostles' Creed as described in the text for Day 3.
    - ❐ Where is Gnosticism found in Christianity today?
- Explore the meaning of *creed* and appropriate uses for the Apostles' Creed.
    - ❐ Consider that it was used as a way to initiate or teach new Christians in the early church.

- [ ] What does it mean to profess a creed, especially one as ancient as the Apostles' Creed, when the meanings of words change over the centuries?
- [ ] How is this creed different from other creeds commonly used in the service of worship?
- [ ] What distinguishes a "confessional" church from a "non-confessional" church?
- Explore how saying the Apostles' Creed with others in a service of worship provides an entry for us, individually and as a community, into the communion of saints.

  - [ ] What difference does it make that we say this creed together, with one voice? What is this story we enter when we say "I believe"?

GATHERING ACTIVITIES
- To begin this session, have the group name creeds and confessions, such as the Nicene Creed or the Westminster Confession. Then have them turn to Deuteronomy 26:5–9. Read it aloud together.

  - [ ] How do these verses function as a creed or confession?
- Ask the group to list features of Gnosticism based on the text for Day 3. Write their ideas on newsprint. Then, looking at the Apostles' Creed, note where it refutes any of those features.

GUIDING THE DISCUSSION
- Three decades or so ago this quote from the *Peanuts* comic strip made the round of posters and sweatshirts: "It doesn't matter what you believe, as long as you're sincere." Ask the group to debate the appropriateness of this statement for a confessional church (refer to the text for Day 6).

- Present a description of the gnostic beliefs that were prevalent at the time the Apostles' Creed was prepared. Refer to the text for Day 3; also consult a dictionary of religion or an encyclopedia. Allow time for the group to ask questions for clarification.

- Have the group identify religious ideas today that are the same as or similar to the concepts of Gnosticism.

- Together identify ways the Apostles' Creed presents the story of the Christian faith in order to counter the gnostic beliefs. During this discussion, point out the use of the creed as a baptismal creed. Also note that the Bible is not mentioned in the Apostles' Creed. What other areas critical to our faith are absent?

- Central to the Apostles' Creed is the recognition that it is a statement of the church, one that brings together that community of faith across the centuries. Ask the following: "How does one think differently about saying the Apostles' Creed when the context is the community of faith and not primarily an individual or personal creed?" As you talk about the Apostles' Creed as the church's creed, include the concepts of the creed as a way the church tells its story, as an act of worship, and as a way to enter the story of the Christian church. Are there other functions for the Apostles' Creed?

- Say the Apostles' Creed together. Be sure everyone has a copy of the creed, even if they memorized it years ago. Write personal creeds: As an ongoing activity, provide time for group members to write their own creeds or credos during or at the end of each session. While it is important to speak the church's creed together, we grow spiritually when we attempt to articulate our individual understanding of the faith. For this session, ask the participants to list the topics or concepts from the Apostles' Creed that seem most important to them today, recognizing that such a list would probably change as their life circumstances change.

Concluding the Discussion

- Sing a hymn: Sing or read a hymn that professes the Christian faith, such as "We All Believe in One True God" (*The Presbyterian Hymnal*, no. 137).

- Conclude with prayer. Give thanks for the words of the Apostles' Creed and for Christians, through the years and today, who seek to understand them and live them.

Notes:

SMALL GROUP STUDY
For discussion of Days 8–14 in the daily reader;
to be used after Day 14

*S*ession
2

"I Believe in God . . . the Father Almighty"

SESSION FOCUS

We confess God, the father of Jesus Christ, to be the one who exercises power through benevolent care, and whose love creates all that is and that shall be.

MAIN IDEAS

When Christians use "father" to address God, it modifies "almighty" from within a biblical context, and, at the same time, the almightiness of God modifies "father." If, however, we understand the name "father" (whether we use it for God or not) to name the relationship between God and Jesus, and, therefore, between God and us, we understand that this God lives in a relation of love to Jesus, and thus to the world. This God created and creates all that is of love. Finally and joyously, this is the God whom we trust.

PREPARING TO LEAD

- Read the daily reader, Days 8–14.

- Plan to explore what it means for group members to call God "father." Spend time on this during the discussion rather than glossing over it. The purpose of the discussion is to bring out the range of experiences and understandings rather than to convince everyone to think the same way or to pronounce the "politically correct" way to speak of God. If necessary, plan to have participants read provocative statements from the text for Day 11 and discuss the statements.

- Explore the meaning of "Father almighty."

  ❑ Plan to ask the group members how they connect "Father almighty" to the person of Jesus Christ. The writer moves from the relation between "Father almighty" and Jesus to God as love. Invite the group to describe how that leap helps them interpret the Apostles' Creed.

i*B*elieve

65

❑ Consider these questions: How is the creation by God a theme of the creed? Why might this have been important to the writers of the creed? What meaning does it have for contemporary Christians?

GATHERING ACTIVITIES
(Use these suggestions whenever they seem appropriate.)
- Create a list of important words. Provide participants with a copy of the Apostles' Creed and hand out colored pens or pencils. Have them underline up to 20 words that they find the most important. When they finish, have them sit with a partner and combine their lists, so they still have no more than 20 words. Continue doing this until the entire group has created one list of 20 words. Then look at the list together and ask the following: "What features of our faith are represented in this list?" "What does it omit that you find essential?"

- Invite the group to recall names for God that are found in Scripture, that they have heard in worship, or that they use themselves.

GUIDING THE DISCUSSION
- Begin the session by having the group read the first two lines of the Apostles' Creed in unison.

- Have the group read the rest of the creed silently with this question in mind: "After the first two lines, what do we learn about God from this creed?" After the participants have had a chance to examine the creed, ask for their answers to the question, looking for attributes of God in what they say. When they have finished, point out the particular attributes you heard named.

- Refer to the text for Day 10 to discuss the views of Marcion, who was declared a heretic. Some members of your group are likely to have uttered (or thought) words about God that would have had them tried for Marcion's heresy. On that premise, take time to go over why this view is considered heretical. Then ask the following: "How does the view of God presented in the Apostles' Creed move believers away from such views?"

- The author uses "Father almighty" to connect God with Jesus. Ask the group to consider how this connection works for them. What other ways can be used to connect God with Jesus? What does this relationship of love mean for our faith and discipleship?

- Read the Apostles' Creed together. Then invite the participants to name the new understandings of God, Jesus, or the Holy Spirit from this study.

- Conclude with prayer. Give thanks for the words of the Apostles' Creed and for Christians, through the years and today, who seek to understand them and live them.

Optional Activities

- Sing a hymn: Sing or read together a hymn that celebrates the Trinity, such as "We All Believe in One True God" (*The Presbyterian Hymnal,* no. 137) or "God Is One, Unique and Holy" (*The Presbyterian Hymnal,* no. 135). How does the hymn give you the basics of the Christian faith as described in the Apostles' Creed?

NOTES:

SMALL GROUP STUDY
For discussion of Days 15–21 in the daily reader;
to be used after Day 21

$\mathcal{S}$ession 3

"I Believe in God . . . The Crucified Messiah"

SESSION FOCUS

The church confesses that its Lord is a human Messiah, who announced the presence (and coming) of God's reign, and "was crucified, died, and was buried."

MAIN IDEAS

In the Apostles' Creed, Jesus' solidarity with us is emphasized through the phrases "born of the Virgin Mary, suffered under Pontius Pilate." Like us, he was born; he lived in a particular time and place; and he was a person, with all the attributes of humanity. Of course, he was more than this. This Jesus is the one whom we confess as the Messiah, the one announcing the reign of God that was not only coming but is already present. His death was not so much the fate of his humanity (which, of course, it included) as the occasion for the confession of his divine sonship. How he died is not to be overlooked, for it reminds us that his life and deeds were sufficient to have him tried and crucified. Thus, the scandal and wonder of the cross are that this one is Lord, and so disclose God as present in the very places where God is absent.

PREPARING TO LEAD

- Read the daily reader, Days 15–21.
- Explore the name of Jesus and the title of Christ.
    - ❑ What does each tell us about this Palestinian Jew?
    - ❑ When we confess to believe in "Jesus Christ," what are we confessing?
    - ❑ Why does this creed focus on the death and resurrection, ignoring Jesus' ministry?
    - ❑ If you were to expand this section, what would you include?

- Explore a variety of understandings when one confesses Jesus.
  - ❑ Reread the text for Day 17.
  - ❑ Take time to explore the writer's points of view of the phrase "born of the Virgin Mary" (Day 17).
  - ❑ Also consider the meaning of *Christ* or *Messiah*. What is behind this title for Jesus? What is implied, but not said?

GATHERING ACTIVITIES

(Use these suggestions whenever they seem appropriate.)

- Write *God's Only Son, Our Lord* at the top of a sheet of paper, such as shelf paper. Have the group create a time line of Jesus' life. The events can be written on the paper or on index cards that are taped below the title. Another way to develop the time line would be for the group to arrange illustrations of Jesus' life in chronological order, using church school teaching pictures. After constructing the time line, ask the following: "How do we as disciples of this Jesus the Christ fulfill the ministry that he has given us?"

- On newsprint, list all the names or titles for Jesus that the group can find in the Gospels. Note the Gospel source(s) for each one. This can be done by assigning one Gospel to each of four groups. What titles are typical of each Gospel? Where is "Son of God" found? What about Jesus' life and ministry do these titles suggest?

GUIDING THE DISCUSSION

- In unison read the section about Jesus in the Apostles' Creed.

- Ask the following: "If this creed were our only source, what would we know about Jesus?" "Why do you think these things were most important to the writers of the creed?" Refer again to the gnostic beliefs of the time. Have the group compare this section in the Apostles' Creed to the statements about Jesus in A Brief Statement of Faith, the most recent statement of the Presbyterian Church (U.S.A.),

iBelieve

or another contemporary creed. Ask the group to consider these questions: "What in our context made other information about Jesus important to add?" "How do the contemporary creeds speak to our culture and time?"

- Discuss the theories of Jesus' death and resurrection included in the the text for Day 19. Which theory is dominant in the Apostles' Creed? Which theory is dominant in the contemporary creed used in the previous activity?

- Read aloud Philippians 2:6–11. How does this pre-Pauline hymn help us interpret the Apostles' Creed?

- Ask three people to read aloud the following confessions concerning Jesus found in the New Testament: the confessions of Thomas (John 20:24–29), Martha (John 11:17–27), Peter (Luke 9:18–22). Allow time between each reading for the participants to meditate on that person's confession. Then ask the following: "What knowledge of Jesus is each person confessing?"

- Conclude with a time for the participants to reflect on what it means for them to call Jesus Lord and Messiah, asking this question: "What knowledge of Jesus do you confess?" Invite a member of the group to pray.

OPTIONAL ACTIVITIES

- Read a children's book, *The Story of Ruby Bridges* by Robert Coles. This story, referenced in the text for Day 16, is a powerful description of a personal belief in Jesus, even more powerful when you realize that this confession of Jesus is by a child.

- Sing or read hymns of the despair we recognize on Good Friday, as we remember the crucifixion of Jesus. Two appropriate selections are "Were You There?" (*The Presbyterian Hymnal*, no. 102) and "O Sacred Head, Now Wounded" (*The Presbyterian Hymnal*, no. 98). After each hymn, ask: "How does the hymn put us in touch with the knowledge that Jesus was fully human and suffered human pain?"

- Create a rhythm poem: Have the group turn to Philippians 2:6–11. These verses are assumed to have been a hymn of the early church, even before Paul. Together, create a rhythm or beat to which you say the hymn together. Try several rhythm patterns. If this will take too much time, recruit a group member to work out a rhythm for this hymn in advance and teach it to the group.

Notes:

iBelieve

SMALL GROUP STUDY
For discussion of Days 22–28 in the daily reader;
to be used after Day 28

*S*ession 4

"I Believe in . . . the Resurrected Jesus"

SESSION FOCUS
It is the resurrected Jesus that Christians confess as Lord and Savior.

MAIN IDEAS
In the previous session, Jesus was recognized as a human person who suffered and died. In this session, Jesus is confessed as the risen or resurrected Messiah. However, his resurrection is not solely of a divine essence, but of a human person. It is a bodily resurrection. The resurrection indicates Jesus' continuing reign as the human Messiah. This is the work of God, who in Jesus' human person saves. Thus, since the Risen One has ascended to God, humanity is already with God. As the Messiah reigns, thus ushering the reign of God into our present, believers wait in hope for the final judgment. This judgment comes from the Jesus whose way is the reign of God's love. It is, in short, this God whom we confess, the God who is incarnate in Jesus of Nazareth, Jesus the Christ.

PREPARING TO LEAD
- Read the daily reader, Days 22–28.

- Explore the concept of resurrection. Others in the New Testament (Lazarus, Dorcas, the widow's daughter) were brought back from death or resuscitated. What is different about the resurrected Jesus? Again, what is significant about the times that influenced the writing of the Apostles' Creed and the casting of the community's belief in these words? What is significant about the bodily resurrection of Jesus for Christians today?

- Explore these lines of the statement about Jesus Christ in the Apostles' Creed: "He is seated at the right hand of the Father, and he will come again to judge the living and the dead."

What is significant about being seated at the right hand of God? How might the pending judgment of Jesus Christ be a sign of hope? What is the hard lesson in these words? How does this section of the Apostles' Creed catapult us into the reign of God as an event of the future? What difference does that make for us?

GATHERING ACTIVITIES
(Use as appropriate.)
- Working in pairs, have the participants write a haiku poem about the risen Christ. Encourage them to use metaphors. The format for haiku is as follows:

  Line 1: five syllables
  Line 2: seven syllables
  Line 3: five syllables

- As a group, create counterarguments for the theory of the resurrection. Begin by having the participants suggest arguments against the resurrection of Jesus Christ, contemporary or ancient, as you list them on newsprint. When they have exhausted their ideas, have each participant select one argument and pretend it was spoken to him or her by a confirmation student. How would they respond? Follow up the individual reflection with a group discussion or compare thoughts in small groups.

GUIDING THE DISCUSSION
- In unison read the creed (Day 22).
- In the text for Day 24 the raising of Lazarus is called a resuscitation, which is different from the raising or resurrection of Jesus. Ask the group, "What do you see as the differences?" In the Apostles' Creed, we say we believe in "the resurrection of the body." Ask the following: "How does this connect with Jesus' resurrection?" "How does Jesus' resurrection affect our participation in communion?" Some Christian bodies still do

not practice open communion, inviting to the Lord's Table only those people who have the same understanding of the presence of Christ in communion as they do.

- As difficult as the idea of the resurrection may be for Christians after two millenniums, no less difficult is the concept of judgment found in the last phrase of the Apostles' Creed that describes our belief in Jesus Christ. Ask the participants for their initial reactions. Then ask them how they understand the phrase as a sign of hope. Some group members may have been in religious groups who see Jesus as a strict judge, basing this interpretation on Matthew 5:17ff. A conversation of this nature was reported in *The Other Side*. After attending worship with a college classmate from a Christian college that dealt strongly in the judgmental side of Jesus, the writer reports:

> [The Episcopal priest] says to the congregation, "If you want to know God's will for your life, I'll tell you."
>
> He moves to the right section of the church. "Okay, from this aisle over, here is God's will for you: Be neighborly."
>
> He moves to the left. "From this aisle over, here is God's will for you: Love your neighbor."
>
> Facing the center. "Love one another."
>
> I turn to Jan. "Did we ever hear that?"
>
> She shakes her head slowly, eyes on the priest.
>
> "No, sister, no. We did not."

- What have these two parishioners discovered about judgment and hope?
- In unison read the entire section about Jesus Christ in the Apostles' Creed. Offer a closing prayer.

iBelieve

OPTIONAL ACTIVITIES

- Lead a guided meditation: Help the group imagine Jesus Christ coming to them. Have the participants sit comfortably, feet flat on the floor, eyes closed. Explain that you are going to read a Bible passage and suggest that they put themselves into the story and listen as Jesus speaks directly to them. Read John 20:24–29. Then suggest that they continue to imagine themselves in the scene, allowing the action to continue. After a few minutes, ask them to leave the scene in their imaginations and return to the present.

- Sing an Easter hymn: Sing or read a hymn such as "Jesus Christ Is Risen Today" (*The Presbyterian Hymnal*, no. 123) or "Christ Is Risen" (*The Presbyterian Hymnal*, no. 109), rejoicing that Jesus was resurrected. What view of the resurrection does the hymn reveal?

NOTES:

SMALL GROUP STUDY
For discussion of Days 29–35 in the daily reader;
to be used after Day 35

*S*ession
5

"I Believe in God . . . the Holy Spirit"

SESSION FOCUS
We will study the way in which the Holy Spirit is God's presence with God's pilgrim people.

MAIN IDEAS
The Holy Spirit is "God with us." The Reformed notion of the "internal testimony" of the Spirit is the "place" where we begin, and thus can utter the creed. God draws us into the story; the Spirit turns these stories about God into stories of God for us. Thus God-with-us, through the church as the act of God gathering forgiven sinners, is present beyond death to eternal life. The Apostles' Creed tilts against a false separation of "spirit" from the created reality, affirming the created order. The "resurrection of the body" reminds us that God created us as body and soul and called this creation good.

PREPARING TO LEAD
- Read the daily reader, Days 29–35.
- Explore the notion that the presence of the Holy Spirit makes belief possible.
    - ❏ How do we attain belief?
    - ❏ Can you describe the origins of your belief?
    - ❏ What set of events converged to that point in your life where you could speak the creed out loud and in public? (See the last paragraph of "God Within," Day 31.)
    - ❏ What is the role of the Holy Spirit in bringing us to this moment?
- Explore your understanding of Spirit—God's Spirit, the Holy Spirit.
    - ❏ What are your first connections with the Spirit?
    - ❏ What do you expect a "Spirit-filled congregation" to look like or act like?

iBelieve

☐ How can we interpret the Holy Spirit as God-with-us?
☐ Read all or some of the following Bible passages: Matthew 28:20, Ephesians 2:8, John 14:15–17, Romans 8:38–39. Although these references are all from the New Testament, God's Spirit (*ruach*) is also central in the Hebrew Scriptures. The Holy Spirit did not come into being on Pentecost.

GATHERING ACTIVITIES

(Use these suggestions whenever they seem appropriate.)

• On newsprint, write: *I believe in God, the Holy Spirit.* Invite the participants to interpret or expand on the meaning of this sentence. If they are hesitant, suggest that they review the text for Days 30–35.

• Write the following lines from A Brief Statement of Faith on newsprint, or make photocopies to distribute to the group:

> We trust in God the Holy Spirit,
> everywhere the giver and renewer of life.
> The Spirit justifies us by grace through faith,
> sets us free to accept ourselves and to love God
> and neighbor,
> and binds us together with all believers
> in the one body of Christ, the Church.

• Have the participants look for connections between the above and the statements about the Holy Spirit in the text for Day 32.

GUIDING THE DISCUSSION

• Distribute paper and pencils or pens. Suggest that the group members read the last paragraph in "God Within" (Day 31) and prepare their own faith history, paying particular attention to what prompted their faith development (e.g., events, people, questions, Scripture, etc.). Assure them that this exercise is to help them recall how God's story has been presented to them and by whom. They can reveal only what they wish in the group discussion.

- Together discuss the role of the Holy Spirit in faith maturity. Encourage the group members to speak of their personal faith histories. They may not have identified the work of the Spirit specifically. Thus, you might refer to the text for Days 31 and 32. Affirm the varieties of ways that the Holy Spirit works in us and through us to call others to God. This discussion may turn toward the meaning of conversion, but don't allow it to derail the rest of your session plan.

- Turn now to the Apostles' Creed to look at the cluster of beliefs that are part of the"I believe in the Holy Spirit" sentence.
  - ❏ Ask: "What threads connect these concepts?"
  - ❏ Focus on the phrase "the forgiveness of sins": Is it in the wrong place in the creed? Why or why not?
  - ❏ Have the group recite in unison the "I believe in the Holy Spirit" sentence. Then ask: "Once we have spoken together this section of the Apostles' Creed, how does it affect us?" "What is the continuation of the story for twenty-first century Christians?" Refer the participants to the text for Day 35, focusing on the passages pertaining to body and soul and life everlasting.

- Conclude the session by reading the Apostles' Creed together. Read it slowly, pausing after each line in the section beginning with "I believe in the Holy Spirit" to allow time for meditation.

- Offer a closing prayer.

Optional Activities

- Create symbols: Provide paper (all kinds), cardboard boxes (all sizes and shapes), glue, scissors, and any other craft materials you wish. Have groups of two or three people each create symbols for the Holy Spirit. Place their creations on a table or the floor in the middle of the group. Rather than have the creators explain or describe their work, invite the participants to interpret what they see.

- Sing a hymn: Sing or read a hymn about the Holy Spirit, such as "Spirit of the Living God" (*The Presbyterian Hymnal*, no. 322) or "Loving Spirit" (*The Presbyterian Hymnal*, no. 323). Which descriptions of the Holy Spirit in the hymn resonate with your discussion about the readings for this session? What theology of the Holy Spirit is dominant in the hymn?

Notes:

NOTES:

NOTES: